Capuchin Monkey Aides

Judith Janda Presnall

**KIDHAVEN
PRESS**™

THOMSON

™

GALE

San Diego • Detroit • New York • San Francisco • Cleveland
New Haven, Conn. • Waterville, Maine • London • Munich

THOMSON

GALE

Cover: © David H. Wells/CORBIS
© Andrea Campbell, 20, 38
© Najlah Feanny/CORBIS, 14, 16, 19
© Wolfgang Kaehler/CORBIS, 7
Brandy Noon, 5
© Jeffrey L. Rotman/CORBIS, 6, 9, 11, 23, 25, 26, 28, 31, 35, 36
© David H. Wells/CORBIS, 10, 13, 32

© 2003 by KidHaven Press. KidHaven Press is an imprint of The Gale Group, Inc.,
a division of Thomson Learning, Inc.

KidHaven™ and Thomson Learning™ are trademarks used herein under license.

For more information, contact
KidHaven Press
27500 Drake Rd.
Farmington Hills, MI 48331-3535
Or you can visit our Internet site at http://www.gale.com

LIBRARY OF CONGRESS CATALOGING-IN-PUBLICATION DATA

Presnall, Judith Janda.
  Capuchin Monkey Aides / by Judith Janda Presnall.
    p. cm. — (Animals with jobs)
Summary: Discusses the monkey as an unusual helper companion, training,
and on the job.
Includes bibliographical references and index.
  ISBN 0-7377-1788-2 (hardback : alk. paper)
1. Monkeys as aides for people with disabilities—Juvenile literature.
2. Capuchin monkeys—Juvenile literature. 3. Quadriplegics—Rehabilitation—
Juvenile literature. [1. Monkeys as aides for people with disabilities.
2. Monkeys—Training. 3. Capuchin monkeys. 4. Quadriplegics—Rehabilitation.
5. People with disabilities—Rehabilitation.] I. Title. II. Series.
  HV1569.6.P74 2003
  362.4'383—dc21
                                                    200215392

Printed in the United States of America

Contents

OCT   2005

Chapter One

Unusual Helpers

The capuchin (ka-pyoo-chin) monkey looks surprisingly human with its big and intelligent eyes. But its hands are the most amazing of all. The small monkey's hands, fingers, and thumbs look and function just like a human's.

Monkeys in Service

Because of their tiny, **dexterous** hands, and helpful attitude, capuchins are well suited as helpers to people who are severely **disabled**. They are especially helpful to **quadriplegics**, people who cannot use their arms and legs.

A quadriplegic's spinal cord has been damaged to the point that the nerves can no longer send messages to the brain to move the limbs. Quadriplegics spend their days mostly in wheelchairs. Capuchins can restore some sense of **independence** and **dignity** for quadriplegics as well as offer affection.

Using their humanlike fingers, monkey helpers perform many simple tasks for the disabled person. For example, the capuchins can unscrew a jar lid, pick up items as tiny as a piece of thread or as large as a magazine, and insert cassettes or CDs. They also fetch food and drinks from a refrigerator. They turn lights on or off, scratch an itch for their companions, and even comb their hair.

The presence of an affectionate capuchin monkey relieves the hours of loneliness that quadriplegics sometimes feel. Most importantly, the monkey allows the quadriplegic to achieve a certain level of independence.

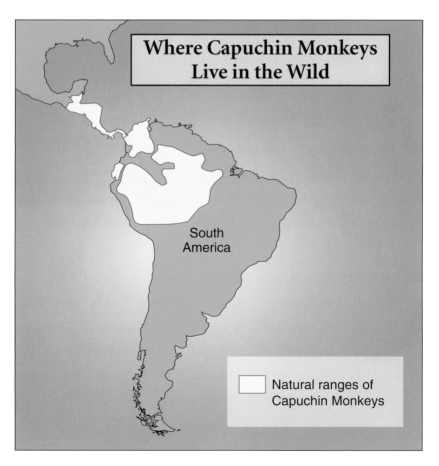

Where Capuchin Monkeys Live in the Wild

South America

Natural ranges of Capuchin Monkeys

A trained capuchin monkey helps its physically challenged owner insert a cassette into a tape player.

Why Capuchin Monkeys?

Capuchins are among the most intelligent and friendly of monkeys. They range in size from thirteen to twenty-two inches long and weigh between three and eleven pounds. Their tails are about the same length as their small bodies. Female capuchins are more suitable as helpers than male capuchins because they are more controllable and bite less readily.

These tiny helpers can live for thirty to forty years, and can be of service for a long time. In comparison, a guide dog, trained to help the blind, has a life span of about ten years. And it costs the same amount ($25,000) to train the dog as it does to train a capuchin. The idea to train monkeys for this task is relatively new—it first began in 1977.

A white-faced capuchin monkey rests on a branch. Capuchin monkeys have humanlike hands, fingers, and thumbs.

An Idea in the Making

Dr. Mary Joan Willard was a behavioral psychologist and assistant professor of **rehabilitation** medicine at the Boston University School of Medicine when she **befriended** a quadriplegic named Joe, who was left severely **paralyzed** after a car accident. Dr. Willard began visiting Joe every day. She brushed his hair, brought him drinks, put cassettes in his tape player, and performed other easy tasks.

Dr. Willard knew about research involving animal learning. She believed that an intelligent animal with "hands" could be trained to do repetitive tasks for quadriplegics. Her first thought for such an animal was a chimpanzee.

However, because an average chimpanzee weighs 150 to 200 pounds, Dr. Willard believed it would be too difficult for a quadriplegic to handle or control. She eventually realized that the small capuchin monkey was a better choice for her project.

At first, Dr. Willard tried training older capuchins. Some people donated their pet monkeys, and others were obtained from zoos. Dr. Willard soon discovered, however, that these capuchins did not completely trust humans. Instead, she decided that having humans raise capuchins from infancy would work best.

Moving Forward

Dr. Willard's biggest obstacle was obtaining money for her project. "I looked everywhere for [financial] support," she told a reporter. "You would be amazed at people's

Having humans raise baby capuchin monkeys teaches them to trust and be comfortable with people.

reactions. They said it would be **demeaning** to use monkeys in the program. Some said that it was sickening, that it would make the world laugh."[1] After two years and thirty-eight rejections, Dr. Willard finally received a **grant** from the Paralyzed Veterans of America.

Colleague Judi Zazula, a rehabilitation engineer and **occupational therapist**, had joined Dr. Willard in pursuing the monkey-helper idea. Zazula worked in the training center. She also screened human applicants and helped capuchin monkeys and clients adjust to each other.

First Monkey Helper Assigned

In 1979, Robert Foster from Watertown, Massachusetts, was the first quadriplegic to receive a monkey helper. The three-year-old female capuchin, named Hellion, fed her twenty-five-year-old owner daily. Hellion opened, closed, and locked doors with a key, she turned lights on and off, and she moved small objects from one place to another.

But when Robert was reading or watching television, Hellion became mischievous. The monkey overturned wastebaskets, scattered the trash, and knocked over objects around the house. She had to learn that certain household objects were off limits. Hellion was returned to the center for additional training.

Robert Foster gets help from his capuchin monkey companion, Hellion.

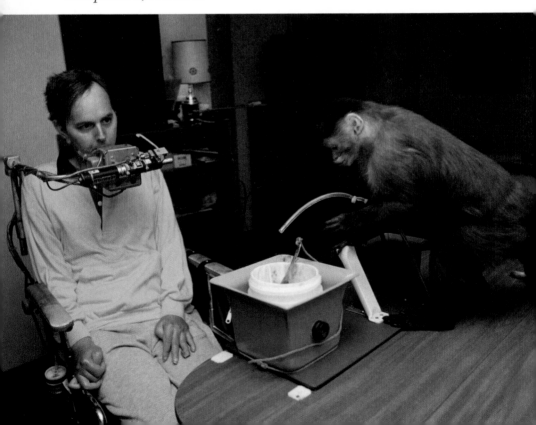

Skepticism Faces Capuchin Helpers

In 1981, scientists were still skeptical that capuchin monkeys could be used to assist quadriplegics. But Dr. Willard was not discouraged. "We think our work could have a significant impact on the daily lives of those who have a real need to supplement the help that is provided by human and mechanical [such as electric wheelchairs] means,"[2] she said. Thus, Dr. Willard continued working on her project. The following year, she founded Helping Hands: Simian Aides for the Disabled.

Today, more than twenty years later, a total of sixty capuchins have been assigned to quadriplegics all over the United States. Judi Zazula conducts a thorough **evaluation** of each applicant. "Not all quadriplegics are super people," she says. "A lazy person before an accident will likely be a lazy [unmotivated] paralyzed person."[3] Zazula wants applicants who are energetic and interested.

Before a capuchin is assigned to a quadriplegic, however, it must live with a foster family and undergo formal training. Helping Hands relies on foster homes where caring people are willing to raise a tiny infant capuchin, giving it the same love and care they would give a human newborn.

Chapter Two

Foster Parents to Monkeys

For the first fifteen years, Helping Hands obtained its infant capuchins from a breeding colony on Discovery Island at Disney World's Zoological Park in Orlando, Florida. Around 1994, a new breeding colony was established for Helping Hands at the Bernice and Milton Stern Building at Southwick's Zoo near Boston, Massachusetts. Within this colony, about thirty-five capuchins are born each year.

First Step

The first step in training is teaching the monkey how to **interact** with people. This process, called **socialization**, is undertaken first by handlers at the center and then by a foster family. At age six to eight weeks, infant monkeys leave their breeding grounds and go to live at Boston's Helping Hands facility until they are assigned to a **foster parent**. Since the training center has many handlers, this contact with a variety of humans helps the monkey become more confident with people. Trainers and handlers play with, feed, cuddle, and bathe the tiny capuchins. Then they evaluate each monkey's personality and **character** before matching it to a foster parent.

An infant capuchin monkey is fed using a baby bottle. When this monkey grows older it will be trained by Helping Hands in Boston, Massachusetts.

A Trip to Boston

New foster parents must go to the Helping Hands facility in Boston to pick up their capuchin. Their experience at the training facility helps them learn more about the important job of raising a monkey. They tour the training rooms and come to understand the organization's goals and objectives.

Dr. Willard, the founder of Helping Hands, says to foster parents, "You can't just love animals. You have to give a monkey the full-time attention you would a human baby." [4]

A married couple working as foster parents train a young capuchin monkey, a commitment that can last up to five years.

At the Foster Home

Bringing up a monkey is not an easy task. It can become a five-year **commitment**. At birth, a monkey weighs about nine ounces—the weight of an average-size apple. Infant monkeys are bottle-fed until they are about six months old. Until around the age of one year, they wear diapers whenever they are outside their cages. Helping Hands then gives suggestions on potty training the monkeys in their cages.

A foster parent must be patient and willing to spend at least five or six hours each day with the monkey. The primary foster parent must not work outside the home. It is a full-time job to provide a young monkey with the guidance that it needs.

A capuchin foster parent must be an adult, and there cannot be children under the age of ten living in the foster parent's home. This is because both young children and young monkeys demand much attention. Young children would take the foster parent's attention away from the monkey. Having teenagers in the home, however, is acceptable. They may even help care for the monkey. To keep the monkey out of trouble, it sleeps in a cage at night.

Cage Requirements

The monkey's cage should be placed in the most frequently used room in the house so that the monkey becomes a part of the family's activities. The metal or plastic cage must be at least six feet high, three feet wide, two-and-a-half feet deep, and eighteen inches off the floor.

A capuchin monkey in training eats a monkey biscuit while sitting in the door to its cage.

The special cage needs two doors: a large door to allow the foster parent cleaning access and a smaller door for the monkey to use. The sides of the cage should be made of one-inch-square open mesh material—not chicken wire, which might injure the monkey. It is essential that someone clean the cage daily.

A Foster Mother of Two Capuchins

Despite the time and effort involved in raising a monkey, foster parents agree that it is worth it. Patrice Kindl, who lives in Ballston Lake, New York, is serving as a foster parent to two capuchin monkeys at the same time. She is a writer and works at home. Patrice realizes that it will be difficult to give up her "kids" when the time comes. But she is also proud that they will become an essential part of a disabled person's life.

Patrice's first capuchin, Kandy, weighed less than a pound when she arrived at her house. Patrice remembers all the work involved in caring for the tiny monkey: "I got up in the middle of the night to feed her. I made formula, changed diapers, [and] did a lot of laundry." [5]

When Patrice works at her computer, she keeps both Kandy and Susi, her second and older capuchin, near her. She keeps both monkeys on twenty-foot leashes so that she can keep track of them. Patrice, her husband, and their seventeen-year-old son "tickle [Kandy and Susi], kiss them, hug them, play with them—all the things you do with a child," [6] she explains.

Patrice's Routine with Her Monkeys

Patrice starts the day at 9:00 A.M., bringing breakfast to the two monkeys in their cages. The menu varies. In foster homes, and at the training center, older capuchins eat about ten to twenty walnut-size monkey biscuits a day. In addition, they eat half an orange and a handful of grapes (their favorite). Other foods may include apple slices, vegetables, high-protein monkey chow, and an occasional hard-boiled egg. Helping Hands monkeys also receive a chewable vitamin pill. The capuchins will sometimes catch and eat insects in the house, such as flies that buzz around them.

After breakfast, Patrice bathes the capuchins in the kitchen sink. Afterward, the two monkeys may groom each other by picking through their fur for dried skin. Sometimes the monkeys enjoy watching people from the window.

Kandy likes to help with household chores. She holds onto the broom when Patrice sweeps the floor. She also "washes" windows, using a paper towel in one hand while leaving handprints all over the glass with her other hand. Although not a required part of caring for a young monkey, the foster parents have taught Kandy and Susi to come, fetch, and put an object in a container. At 10:00 P.M., the monkeys are put back into their cages for about an eleven-hour sleep.

Ziggy's Day

Andrea Campbell of Hot Springs Village, Arkansas, applied to be a foster parent to a capuchin monkey. She was excited to learn that, out of three thousand applicants, she was one of two hundred chosen. When her female monkey Ziggy was very young, she wanted to be in close contact with Andrea at all times. It was common for Andrea to perform her everyday activities such as vacuuming,

Foster parent Patrice Kindl teaches Kandy, her capuchin monkey, to hold an ink pen.

Andrea Campbell has been a capuchin monkey foster parent since 1989, and even wrote a book about her experiences training Ziggy (pictured).

dusting, walking, and typing with Ziggy clinging to her wrist sound asleep.

As a capuchin grows older, foster parents will likely experience many bites. To guard against severe biting, foster parents return their monkeys to Helping Hands to have their front teeth removed when they are about three years old. The monkeys are still able to eat their usual food with their back teeth, and their biscuits are softened with water.

Outdoor Activities

Capuchins wear a leash when they accompany their human caretakers outside the house. When Andrea took a walk or rode her bicycle, Ziggy, attached by a leash, rode on the back of Andrea's head with one leg on each side of her ears. Another foster parent says that her monkey likes to ride on her dog's back when they go for walks.

During the years a person serves as a foster parent, a strong bond develops between family members, household pets, and the capuchin. But when a monkey reaches adulthood—about the age of five years—it must be returned to Helping Hands for advanced training.

Chapter Three

Training: Monkey See, Monkey Do

A dvanced training at the Boston Helping Hands center lasts six to twelve months. During this time, the monkey must learn many tasks that help a quadriplegic. It will again interact with many handlers, people who feed, bathe, and play with the monkeys.

Training Sessions

Although the monkey has contact with several handlers, it will have only one trainer. Five or six times a week, the trainer works with the monkey in sessions that last thirty to forty-five minutes. However, each monkey learns at its own pace. The length of a training session depends on the intellect and willingness of the individual capuchin.

Trainers often get grimy during the sessions. According to one trainer, "You can't be afraid to get down on the floor and get dirty. Monkeys will get food all over you."[7]

The First Training Room

Training takes place in three rooms. The first room is about the size of a walk-in closet. The **soundproof** room helps the monkey concentrate on learning the necessary tasks without distractions. And low-level lighting helps the monkey see a laser light, a dime-size movable red spot projected from a thin flashlight.

During practice, the monkey must first get used to seeing the red light cast on different items without trying to

A Helping Hands trainer teaches a monkey to retrieve objects by using a red laser light.

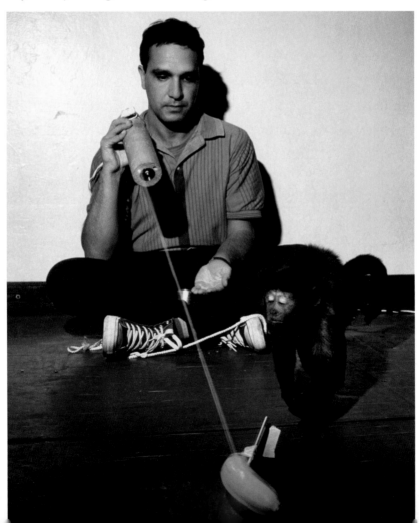

catch and eat the dot. Next, the trainer shines the laser dot on one small bottle within a group of three bottles and tells the monkey to fetch it. If the monkey chooses the correct bottle and brings it to the trainer, it is rewarded with a grape. This lesson is repeated multiple times.

Also in this room, the monkey learns to touch a red-painted block that is glued to a board. The red color represents the red laser light that the monkey will later learn to recognize as a requested item from the quadriplegic.

A few things in this first small training room, such as a plant or framed picture, have white quarter-size dots pasted on them. The monkey learns that these items are off limits. If the monkey does not touch them, sometimes it receives a reward such as food. This lesson is intended to teach the monkey what it must leave alone once it becomes a helping companion to a quadriplegic. Before the monkey arrives, white dots will be applied to treasured objects in the person's home.

Other Training Rooms

The second training room is about the size of a small bathroom. In this room, the trainer and monkey work with real equipment, such as light switches, cassette machines, drink holders, and even a microwave oven.

The third room is larger and not soundproof. It represents a quadriplegic's home. The room has a hospital bed and a wheelchair, a lamp, a telephone, and other household items, as well as a monkey cage. Trainers have marked some items found there with the "don't touch" white stick-on dots.

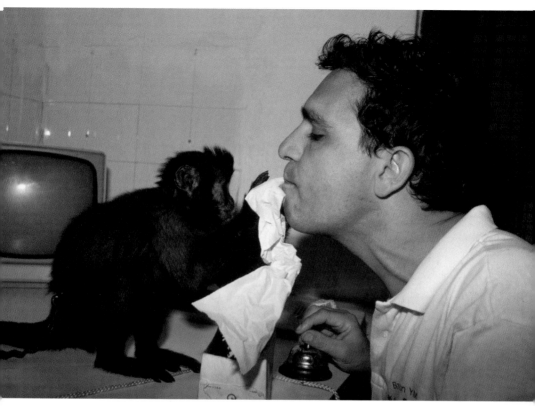

A capuchin monkey is taught to wipe someone's mouth with a napkin.

Putting Lessons into Practice

The capuchin's final lessons take place in the third room. In this room, a trainer sits in a wheelchair pretending to be a quadriplegic. The monkeys here are taught to ride on some part of the wheelchair or on the person's lap. The trainer instructs the monkey to fetch a drink. The monkey should leave the wheelchair, open the mini refrigerator, retrieve a drink, and bring it to the trainer.

Once the monkey has brought the drink to the trainer, they ride together to a desk area. (Most quadriplegics move their wheelchairs with the aid of a chin control or by blowing into a mouthpiece, which propels the wheeled vehicle.) The monkey learns to put the drink on the desk, open it, and place a straw in it. If the monkey performs correctly, the trainer squeezes a bulb that is mounted on the wheelchair. The bulb dispenses a sip of fruit drink as a

During the last stages of its training a capuchin monkey switches on a light.

reward. At this point, the monkey is on its way to becoming an official "helping hand."

Training Methods: Verbal Commands

Monkeys learn the same way children do: by watching and imitating. A beginning lesson involves learning to fetch or to pick up a simple object. The trainer shows the monkey what is expected and then calls the monkey's name and says "Do this!"

For example, the trainer might want the monkey to retrieve an object and place it in a box. Learning this task takes several days of training. Next, the trainer will ask for the object to be placed in his or her hand. This step must be performed successfully at least a dozen times on different days before the monkey can move on to a new task.

Monkey Rewards

When the monkey successfully completes a task, trainers reward it with praise, hugs, and a treat, such as a sip of juice or a dab of peanut butter. If a monkey does not do the task properly, it is not punished. It simply does not receive a treat, but it can try again.

Laser Beam

Since quadriplegics cannot use their arms or legs to reinforce their verbal commands to a monkey, they hold a pencil-size laser stick in their mouth to point to objects they want. The laser is about eight inches long and shines a harmless tiny red dot on items to be fetched. Monkeys are taught to respond to the laser light when a quadriplegic shines the light on a needed item.

Learning to serve drinks to a quadriplegic owner is an important lesson for trained capuchin monkey helpers.

Drinking Straws

The capuchins must also learn to serve drinks. First, they learn to insert a straw into a container. They begin practice with a two-inch-long straw, then a four-inch one. As the lesson continues, the straws become progressively longer. The final straw will be a flexible one that is more convenient for the quadriplegic to use.

Ready for an Assignment

Before the monkey can be assigned to a quadriplegic, the capuchin must be able to follow both verbal and laser-beam commands. It needs to know how to fetch items from the floor and the refrigerator. The monkey should also have learned to place magazines on a rack, insert straws into drinks, and place CDs and cassettes into their players. Learning to follow commands to perform simple tasks and providing companionship are the capuchin monkey's basic jobs.

Chapter Four

Capuchins on the Job

A capuchin monkey's assignment is determined by two elements: the tasks the monkey does best and the disabled person's needs. Helping Hands considers both the ability of the person and the **competence** of the monkey.

For example, a particular monkey may not be competent at following verbal commands but may be especially skilled at following the laser beam. This monkey would be assigned to work for a quadriplegic who has speech problems and cannot give verbal commands. In this case the person would blow a whistle attached to the wheelchair to get the monkey's attention before using the laser stick. About halfway through its training, a capuchin will be matched to the person it will assist. In this way, the trainer discovers which tasks the monkey must learn.

A Monkey Aide Arrives

Once a monkey has been properly matched and trained, the placement trainer for Helping Hands escorts the monkey to the home of the disabled person. For two weeks, the trainer will observe the monkey with the quadriplegic to make sure it meets the person's needs. After that, a support person visits the patient daily in order to help the monkey and disabled person develop a regular routine. In about eight weeks, the monkey should be under the quadriplegic's control.

Each capuchin monkey is matched with a disabled owner depending on the abilities of the monkey and the needs of the person.

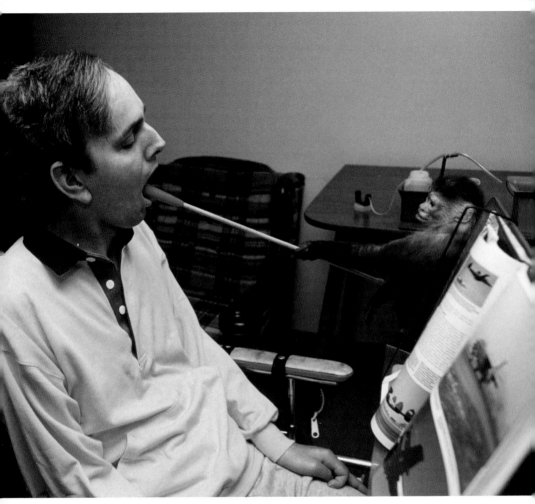

Hellion helps his owner, Robert Foster, replace his mouth-stick.

Greg and Willie

Two years after a diving accident left eighteen-year-old Greg severely disabled, Helping Hands brought him a trained female monkey named Willie. Greg's family put Willie's seven-foot-tall cage in the bedroom where Greg spends most of his time. He has a mini refrigerator there for drinks.

Before Willie arrived, Greg's family marked his furniture and other possessions that were "out of bounds" for Willie with white stick-on dots. Greg's wheelchair was also given some new features: a laser device, a treat dispenser, and a button on a small speaker. This button lets out a high-pitched noise that irritates Willie and makes her stop if she is doing something mischievous.

Willie Practices Skills with Greg

Greg and Willie had to practice a lot together before Willie learned to do everything successfully. One task that Willie does often for Greg is putting his mouth stick back into his mouth when he drops it. Greg uses his rubber-tipped mouth stick for many tasks: to push down computer keys, push cassette player and telephone buttons, change channels on the TV, and turn the pages of a book or magazine.

Greg was delighted with Willie's learning process: "You should have seen Willie while she was learning how to give me my mouth stick. It didn't take her very long to get it right, but sometimes she put it in her own mouth. It was a funny scene!"[8]

Continuing a Career at Home

The mouth stick is a quadriplegic's primary tool. It even helped Sue Strong continue her career. Sue was a librarian before she became paralyzed at age twenty-two following an automobile accident. She now works at home part-time for the Library of the Blind and Physically Handicapped.

Sue is able to do this because she has Henrietta (or Henri, for short) to fetch her mouth stick and do other simple tasks. And because of Henri, Sue can be left alone for several hours in her New York City apartment. The capuchin monkey even does light housekeeping. "She clears away [empty containers], sponges off table-tops, and then stares at her reflection,"[9] Sue says, laughing.

Sue loves Henri's companionship, even though she is mischievous. Sometimes Henri will dim the lights when Sue is reading. The monkey knows that Sue will have to ask her to turn them back up and then she will get a reward. Henri's reward is a thimbleful of sticky, strawberry-flavored juice. Sue dispenses the juice into a cap by blowing into a plastic tube mounted beside her wheelchair headrest.

Wanted: Independence

Like Sue, Gary Finkle can also be left alone for several hours because of his capuchin, Jo. The monkey provides Gary's caretaker wife with some needed freedom. Gary's wife can work afternoons in town without worrying about her quadriplegic husband being at home alone. Gary, who became paralyzed after a swimming pool accident, is self-reliant because of Jo. He treasures Jo's companionship. "The main thing is independence," Gary says. "[Jo's] a constant source of entertainment, and she just keeps getting smarter. The more she's exposed to, the more she learns," he marvels. "I want to teach her to play backgammon."[10]

Monkeys Bring Happiness

Forty-one-year-old Tom, a quadriplegic who has a twenty-year-old capuchin named Mango, expresses the feelings of many other monkey recipients, "Mango makes me happy," he says. "I *am* happy. Mango loves me and I love him. He is my son. When I got him, I sent out birth announcements."[11]

Monkeys Offer Companionship

Eager to get a monkey helper for himself, Kim Torbitt spent two weeks filling out the thirteen-page application. (He operates his computer, one key at a time, using a pencil-like stick attached to the **splint** of his left hand.)

Trained capuchin monkeys can offer affection to their owners as well as perform household tasks.

"It would be wonderful to have the luxury of being able to be more independent," he wrote. "I also would love to have the chance to care for and love a monkey as if it were the child I never had the opportunity to have."[12]

Forty-one-year-old Kim has been paralyzed since he was eighteen. He broke his neck when he was thrown from the passenger seat of a car that was going more than one hundred miles per hour in a drag race.

As a quadriplegic, Kim considers this his second life. Although Kim has twice-daily sessions with a health care aide and visits from his girlfriend, he wanted a companion and helper on a full-time basis. Kim was excited to be accepted into the Helping Hands program.

To relieve his companion's itch a capuchin monkey rubs the woman's face with a cloth.

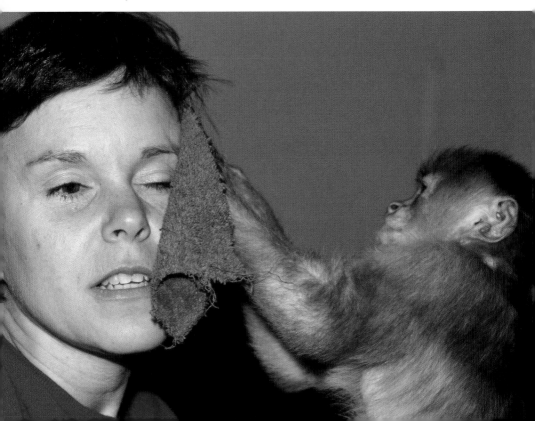

Judi Zazula, Helping Hands' director, brought the female capuchin Mymu to Kim's apartment. After taking several days to become acquainted, Mymu snuggled on Kim's lap. Then she climbed to his shoulder, licked his ear, touched her smooth fingertips to his face, and picked through his hair ("for **cooties** that aren't there," explains Kim). Kim spoke softly to Mymu: "Yes, Mymu, I'm your Daddy. We're going to have a long and happy life together." [13]

When Patients Return Their Capuchins to Helping Hands

Unfortunately, some monkeys must be returned to Helping Hands. This happened to Kim Torbitt. It was like losing a member of his family.

It turned out that Kim was **allergic** to Mymu. Kim developed an itchy rash on his face. When Kim commanded, "Mymu, itch," Mymu rubbed it with a small cloth. The rash became worse as the months passed. Judi Zazula suggested that Kim keep Mymu in her cage for a few days. The rash disappeared.

After thirteen months of companionship, Kim had to return his beloved "child" to Helping Hands. Judi discovered that Mymu had **diabetes** and that perhaps her unique body chemistry had irritated Kim's skin. Mymu had to get **insulin** shots.

Greg, another quadriplegic, had to give up his monkey, named Willie. Greg decided to go to college and live in a dorm. Helping Hands did not think that Willie could be kept in a safe environment on the campus.

Ziggy (pictured), like other capuchin monkeys, help improve the lives of those with physical challenges.

Capuchins usually stay with their paralyzed companion until they can no longer work.

Quadriplegics will always need people to assist them with such things as getting in and out of bed, bathing, and dressing. But having a trained monkey companion lessens their reliance on other people. These small monkeys change the quality of lives and give quadriplegics a sense of independence and dignity.

Just as guide dogs are eyes for the blind and hearing dogs are ears for the deaf, capuchin monkeys serve as hands and feet for quadriplegics.

Notes

Chapter One: Unusual Helpers
1. Quoted in *New Yorker,* "Capuchin Aides," October 18, 1982, p. 45.
2. Quoted in Scherraine Mack, "Novel Help for the Handicapped," *Science,* April 3, 1981, p. 27.
3. Quoted in J. Tevere MacFadyen, "Educated Monkeys Help the Disabled to Help Themselves," *Smithsonian,* October 1986, p. 131.

Chapter Two: Foster Parents to Monkeys
4. Quoted in Mary Johnson and Stephen Brewer, "Will You Be a Monkey's Uncle?" *New Choices,* November 1990, p. 12.
5. Quoted in Linda J. Brown, "Raising Monkeys with a Mission," *Good Housekeeping,* June 1995, p. 22.
6. Quoted in Brown, "Raising Monkeys with a Mission," p. 22.

Chapter Three: Training: Monkey See, Monkey Do
7. Quoted in Suzanne Haldane, *Helping Hands.* New York: Dutton Children's Books, 1991, p. 14.

Chapter Four: Capuchins on the Job
8. Quoted in Haldane, *Helping Hands,* p. 28.
9. Quoted in Kyle Roderick, "Pets That Give More Than Love," *Woman's Day,* April 2, 1991, p. 87.

10. Quoted in MacFadyen, "Educated Monkeys Help the Disabled to Help Themselves," p. 126.
11. Quoted in Andrea Campbell, *Bringing Up Ziggy.* Los Angeles: Renaissance Books, 1999, p. 194.
12. Quoted in Melissa Stanton, "When Kim Met Mymu," *Life,* August 1995, p. 79.
13. Quoted in Stanton, "When Kim Met Mymu," pp. 79–80.

For Further Exploration

Suzanne Haldane, *Helping Hands*. New York: Dutton Children's Books, 1991. A photo essay focusing on a paralyzed teenager and his capuchin monkey. It shows how monkeys are trained to provide help and companionship to people who are disabled.

Nancy E. Krulik, *Animals on the Job*. New York: Scholastic, 1990. Examines animals hard at work, including animals helping police catch criminals, animals starring in movies and circuses, and animals working with people who are blind, deaf, or disabled.

Clare Oliver, *Animals Helping with Special Needs*. New York: Franklin Watts, 1999. Explains how animals such as horses, dogs, dolphins, and monkeys are trained to help people who have special needs, including the handicapped and the elderly.

Index

About the Author

Judith Janda Presnall is an award-winning nonfiction writer. *Capuchin Monkey Aides* is the eighth book in the Animals with Jobs series. Her other books include *Rachel Carson, Artificial Organs, The Giant Panda, Oprah Winfrey, Mount Rushmore, Life on Alcatraz, Animals That Glow, Animal Skeletons,* and *Circuses.* Presnall graduated from the University of Wisconsin in Whitewater. She is a recipient of the Jack London Award for meritorious service in the California Writers Club. She is also a member of the Society of Children's Book Writers and Illustrators. Judith lives in the Los Angeles area with her husband, Lance, and three cats.